The
Reduced History of
FOOTBALL

The story of the world's greatest game squeezed into 90 minutes

Aubrey Ganguly & Justyn Barnes Illustrations by Tony Husband

ANDRE
DEUTSCH

Other titles in the Reduced History series

The Reduced History of Cricket
ISBN 0-233-00126-3

The Reduced History of Golf
ISBN 0-233-00121-2

The Reduced History of Rugby
ISBN 0-233-00122-0

The Reduced History of Tennis
ISBN 0-233-00191-3

The Reduced History of Britain
ISBN 0-233-00190-5

INTRODUCTION

Football, eh! Marvellous. It's also very very old. Even older than Bobby Robson. By our reckoning, some 900 years old (okay, so maybe just about the same age as Sir Bobby).

And what a fun-packed, net-busting, head-scratching, neck-breaking, team-bonding, headline-launching, nation-dividing, dubious decision-making, trophy-laden, money-spending 900 years it's been. How could we possibly cram it all into one book – especially a book as beautifully formed but, let's face it, small, as this one?

Well, fortunately dear reader, that was our problem not yours. We sifted through the parchments and the papers so you don't have to.

Instead, sit back, relax and enjoy the abbreviated (very abbreviated actually) highlights of the world's greatest sport freshly squeezed into 90 minutes (plus a little extra time).

Um… goal!

KICK OFF

Pancakes for goalposts!
Ye olde pancake-tossers invent footballe

Football, or ye olde footballe as it was almost certainly known in the olden days, was first played in England in the 1100s as part of Shrovetide festivities. Ye olde footballe was a free-for-all. Often hundreds of pancake-tossing villagers or townspeople would play and they made the rules up as they went along. The object of the game might be to carry a ball from one end of the village or town to the other, but how you got there was up to you. Rather than trying to deliver Beckham-esque 40-yard passes to a team-mate standing next to the slaughterhouse, most of the kicking was aimed at the backside of the person mad enough to take possession of the ball. It was like a mixture of hurling, American Football and crown green bowling. Only more violent.

Royal spoilsports ban football

At times in the Middle Ages, football was banned in England, Scotland and France by royal decree! Forsooth, check out this, er, never-before-seen, but clearly authentic legal text...

I hereby decree that out of reverence and honour for God and the blessed Mary, eternal virgin, and for the health of ourselves and our ancestors and heirs, that the liberty of playing the game of ye olde footballe shall heretoforth be prohibited upon England's green pastures. I hereby grant to all bishops full power to constrain the aforesaid sport which encourages my subjects to violent acts... and interferes with archery practice. For this reason I desire and firmly command that it shall be legal for the bishops and their successors to enter the homes of men who possess ye studded boots and to take seizin of any footballes found pertaining to this dangerous activity. So there.

By order of the King

IT'S OFFICIAL – FOOTBALL'S EDUCATIONAL! OR SO RICHARD MULCASTER, THE HEADMASTER OF ST PAUL'S SCHOOL IN LONDON BELIEVED IN THE SIXTEENTH CENTURY. THE TEACHERS ALL THOUGHT HE WAS QUITE MAD – 'MAD MULCASTER' THEY CALLED HIM (ER, PROBABLY). MAD MUL WROTE A TREATISE, WHICH IS LIKE A PAMPHLET BUT BIGGER, CLAIMING THAT FOOTBALL PROVIDED NOT ONLY POSITIVE EDUCATIONAL VALUES BUT ALSO THAT IT COULD BE USED TO PROMOTE HEALTH AND STRENGTH. THE REACTION? WELL, NATURALLY EVERYONE THOUGHT HE WAS QUITE MAD, BUT SOON THE PUPILS GREW HEALTHIER AND STRONGER FROM PLAYING FOOTBALL, AND OTHER HEAD-MASTERS AT OTHER POSH ENGLISH SCHOOLS STARTED TO ENCOURAGE THEIR TOFFEE-NOSED PUPILS TO $\longrightarrow$

→ PLAY FOOTBALL TOO. NO PROPER RULES HAD BEEN INVENTED BACK THEN SO AT FIRST, THE SNOOTY BOYS KICKED THE BALL, PICKED IT UP, THREW IT, SAT ON IT AND USED IT AS A HANGING BASKET OUTSIDE THE BOARDING HOUSE WHEN IT GOT PUNCTURED. BUT OVER THE NEXT FEW CENTURIES, THE GAME WAS TAKEN UP BY MORE AND MORE ENGLISH PUBLIC SCHOOLS AND RULES AND REGULATIONS WERE STANDARDISED.

GOD BLESS YOU MR MULCASTER! YOU MAD OLD BEAN...

"Let's play 11 v 11... HOORAH!"

By 1841, football was legal again and those dandies at Eton
introduced the 11-a-side game. The pupils thought it was divine

Dearest Aunt Mabel,

Returned to Eton for the autumn term and we've
started playing a super new game. This afternoon, I
dashed off to the gymnasium for PE. Master Glossop is
normally such a stick in the mud, and we were all
rather dreading another 35-lap race round the Quad.
Instead, he produced a football and we all popped off to
the playing fields. My chum Topper piped up, "What ho,
old man. Why don't we divide into two teams of 11." Old
Glossop thought it was a frightfully good idea, but there
were 23 of us. Luckily, Fatty Briggs had indigestion
after eating eight cream scones at luncheon, so he just
sat and watched. I say, Aunt Mabel, it was awfully good
fun, kicking the ball as hard as we could and crashing
into each other. I was quite the ruffian! And poor old
Wilberforce Wattle had to be
carted off to matron's to get
his head stitched after an
unfortunate collision with
Bingo's elbow.
Anyway, must dash –
Topper's invited Bingo
and I to his dorm to bob
for apples.
Love to Uncle Horatio.

Pip pip,

Bertie

Cambridge rules OK!

After years of anarchic pig's bladder pummelling, men from public and non-public schools met to create the "Cambridge Rules" which formed the basis for future rulifications...

MEETING TO CODIFY LAWS OF FOOTBALL

Trinity College, Cambridge
13 June 1848

Chairman: WR – Prof. W.Rooney, Headmaster, Winchester
Delegates: SG – Prof. S.Gerrard, Head Of Human Sciences, Eton; Sir JW – Sir J.Wilkinson, Knight of the realm and Master Of Physics, Rugby; MO – Prof. M.Owen, Master Of Mathematics, Harrow; DB – Prof. D.Beckham, Master of English Language, Leytonstone Grammar School

MINUTES
RESTARTING PLAY

WR: Raises the first topic of restarting the game when the ball goes out of play – that is beyond the area bounded only by four corner flags.

SG: Suggests a straight throw-in by hand should be taken.

DB: Agrees SG's proposal has merit, but says he has found restarting play by kicking the stationary ball after it goes out of play to be effective.

Sir JW: Has also found kicking most effective.

MO: Favours the straight throw-in.

WR: Feels DB's proposal is too radical at this time and cast his vote for the straight throw-in.

TACKLING OPPONENT

SG: Proposes that players should continue to be allowed to take the ball from an opponent by any means. Advocates holding, pushing, tripping because it's spiffing good fun.

Sir JW: Agrees it is spiffing good fun.

MO, WR, DB: All strongly disagree and WR declares that such practices be prohibited.

CATCHING THE BALL

WR: Proposes that players be allowed their hands only to catch a kick but not run with it.

MO: Suggests WR is a big girl's blouse.

1

The tale of the tape

In 1865, the Football Association was formed and wooden crossbars were soon erected to celebrate...

IN EARLY FA LAWS THE GOAL WAS DEFINED BY TWO NINE-FOOT HIGH UPRIGHTS EIGHT YARDS APART JOINED BY A FLIMSY BIT OF

TAPE. SOON A STURDIER WOODEN CROSSBAR WAS INTRODUCED.

Tricky vicar is first FA cup hero

On 16 March 1872, "The Prince Of Dribblers" Reverend R.W.S Vidal inspires Wanderers FC to a 1-0 win over Royal Engineers in the first-ever FA Cup final. This is a (very) exclusive extract from Vicar Vidal's very next sermon. Verily.

"Verily we were blessed with a bye to the semi-finals of the Football Association Challenge Cup whereupon our foes were Queens Park of Glasgow. Twas a battle to test the noblest of hearts but we won by nil goals to nil for the infidels couldst not afford to stay in London for a replay. Blessed are the meek indeed. Forsooth, in the final match at Kennington Oval before a 2000-strong congregation, we didst face the Royal Engineers. We met their fiery torches of damnation with the sturdy steed of our faith in almighty God (and the finest players to have graduated from England's public schools and universities). This time, a nil-nil win would not be enough. So it came to pass, that I, the 'Prince Of Dribblers', prayed to the Prince Of Peace and he didst say unto me 'Man On'. And thus it came to pass that I didst pass the ball to my brethren M.P. Betts who scored the winner, whereupon I felt the holy spirit leap inside me and I didst cry, 'Geeetttt in theeerre!' Amen."

Hurts like Corinthian spirit!

Early hero Hon A.F.Kinnaird knocks 'em dead!

A century before that charming Vinnie Jones showed what can be achieved by lack of talent and brutality (and that's just his acting – arf!), the robust style of the Hon A.F. Kinnaird, later an Earl and President of the FA, made him a hero of the amateur game. He was known as "the WG Grace of footie" although unlike Grace his facial hair was a vivid red that you could make out from space. Kinnaird played in nine FA Cup finals and earned five winners medals (which not even Vinnie managed).

In those days, hacking was legal, and Kinnaird could be a pretty intimidating opponent. Legend has it that when a player from another team called on Kinnaird's mum she confessed she lived in fear that her son would one day come back from "that horrid rough game" with a broken leg. To which the opposition player legendarily replied: "Don't worry Ma'am, it won't be his own."

That's the (Corinthian) spirit!

Let there be light!
Sheffield hosts the first floodlit match

Some 20,000 spectators were witness to the first "floodlit" game on a cold October night in Sheffield on 14 October 1878. History was made as a match between two local sides at Bramall Lane was played under electric lights. Four big lamps with considerably bigger bulbs than you have in your house were mounted on 30-foot wooden towers and erected in each corner of the ground and powered by electric generators. The fans loved the, ahem, bright idea and subsequent experiments at other grounds were also greeted with enthusiasm by night owls. The first such experiment in London however proved there was still some work to be done as a combination of uneven lighting and high winds illustrated that the system wasn't yet foolproof. Most illuminating… (sorry).

Artisans take t'coop oop north

Blackburn Olympic tradesmen hammer their Old Etonian aristocratic rivals in't 1883 FA Coop final

Eleven years of Southern domination was ended by the plumbers and weavers of Blackburn Olympic, who plumbed and weaved away to become the first team ever to take FA Cup oop north. Top-hatted Old Etonian supporters in the enclosure at Kennington Oval spilt champers and canapés in disbelief as the 1882 winners were beaten 2–1 after extra time. Not even our old pal, Hon. A.F. Kinnaird, hacking his merry way through his ninth and last FA Cup final could deny the lower-class northerners.

"It were a reet good day" said Olympic half-back and trainer Jack Hunter in response to an unfeasibly long question from Lord Garth Of Crook in't bar after the game.

Do not disturb

Arbroath keeper sleeps through Bonny 36-0 thrashing

Arbroath are now a rubbish lower division Scottish league side but their many centenarian fans have always got the memory of that glorious day 118-ish years ago when they thrashed mighty Bon Accord 36–0.

Yes, on 5 September 1885, just seven years after their formation, the Arbroath team set a goalscoring record for a first-class British match. Bon Accord played in their working clothes, didn't have a pair of boots between them and replaced their injured keeper with a half-back who'd never played in goal before... yes, they were a crack unit.

Arbroath winger John Petrie top-scored with 13 goals while their keeper didn't touch the ball once in 90 minutes of highly-competitive first-class football.

In fact, the goalie had such an anonymous game that it was said that afterwards no-one could remember his name. Not even him. But it is possible we've made that bit up...

Women play football. No, really!

Football authorities condemn female footie farrago

In modern times, it's unthinkable
for women to play football, so
imagine the shock of FA bigwigs
back in the olden days of 1895
when a British Ladies Football
Club was formed! These unhinged
fillies played their first match at
Crouch End in North London.
Kitted out in big, heavy skirts,
homemade shinguards and
nightcaps (for some reason) they
belted the pig's bladder around the
park in front of a mere 10,000
spectators. Clearly, there was no
interest in such a distasteful event
and bewhiskered FA chiefs with
their customary wisdom and
foresight dismissed the game as a
"farce". It is only due to their
vision that the fairer sex no longer
embarrass themselves in this way.

13 The descent of man
Darwenian theory in practice

In Darwinian theory, the game of life is just one long battle for survival where only the strongest survive. But in 1898/99 Darwenian players at Lancashire team Darwen strived heroically to prove themselves the weakest in the game of league football.

In 1899, the Lancastrian Darwenians spectacularly achieved their noble aim, finishing bottom of the Second Division (which was the lowest division in those them there days) with an exceptional nine points from 34 games played. They amassed one point from 17 away fixtures, scoring six and leaking 109 goals in the process. Even Loughborough, the second crappiest team in the league, couldn't descend to anywhere near Darwen's level, smashing them 10–0. Despite the fact that Darwen games guaranteed goal action, amazingly they weren't re-elected to the League the following season. One Darwen player almost certainly remarked sadly, "We just haven't evolved as a team."

14 Pretty in Pink

1899/1900: Scots come up looking rosey!

Ah, the Tartan Army… passionate, proud, and um pink. Or at least they were for this Scotland–England encounter. Somehow, crimson-faced Derby-winning racehorse owner Lord Rosebery, who was attending the match, persuaded the Scottish FA to make his team play in his racing colours of primrose and rose (in other words, yellow and pink).

Can you imagine, burly Scottish blokes wearing pink? The next thing you know, they'll be wearing skirts… er, oh.

Having done the trick for Lord Rosebery's horse, it didn't appear to do the Scottish players any harm either as they romped to a 4–1 victory including a hat-trick from the only amateur in their side: centre-forward R.S.McColl.

"Scotland the brave? You have to be brave to wear those colours"

Bank Of Middlesbrough

Date 19th February 1905

£1000.00

No. T8144157

Pay to Sunderland Football Club

In February 1905, fans in the North East were stunned as the first £1,000 transfer fee was paid by Middlesbrough to Sunderland for England international goal machine Alf Common. The average fee for a top player at the time was £400.

215 67 45 81 T

Director

Bank Of Middlesbrough

16 United outcasts cast back in
FA suspend militant Man United stars but player power prevails

Today of course, the FA and Manchester United enjoy a harmonious relationship that is the envy of all. No arguments about releasing players for international duty, random drug testing procedures, nothing. But in August 1909, the FA suspended the whole United team!

The United players had been instrumental in forming the first players union and at first every professional in the country signed up to join. But pressure from FA officials led to players dropping out one after the other until the Old Trafford "Outcasts" stood alone.

United had just won their first FA Cup, but it seemed the very FA whose very FA trophy they had just won would not let them play in the 1909/10 season!

Then Everton player Tim Coleman joined the Outcasts. Soon his Toffee team-mates and then loads of other teams walked out too until the Outcasts became, um, Incasts and the FA were cast out! Eventually, the FA backed down, agreement was reached and so the seeds of long-time harmony were sown…

"We only said we wanted another striker. Now we've got 11…"

West Auckland win "World Cup"!

It were a miner miracle!

How could a team of "sheep-shearers" win an international competition that hadn't been invented yet? Well, West Auckland weren't from a city in a land near a land down under, they were an amateur team of "plucky miners" from a County Durham village.

And the "World Cup", as it was so wrongly named, was staged in Turin at Easter 1909 by British tea merchant Sir Thomas Lipton to celebrate himself being made a Knight Of The Grand Order Of Italy (what's wrong with "The Lipton Cup", eh?). "Surprisingly", the FA wouldn't send the England team, so Lipton invited the "next best team", West Auckland, who happened to be third from bottom of the Northern Amateur league.

The miraculous miners beat Red Star Zurich (like Red Star Belgrade only better), Stuttgart and then Juventus 2–0 in't final to become champions of the "world".

And to prove it were no fluke the lamp-helmetted heroes went back to Italy the following season and defended their title!

18 The Khaki Cup Final

Football soldiers on during First World War...

With the First World War raging on, the 1915 FA Cup final was played out in wet and gloomy conditions at Old Trafford. A 50,000 crowd including thousands of servicemen dressed in khaki uniform watched Sheffield United beat Chelsea 3–0 in perhaps the most depressing Cup final ever. Match over, the crowd dispersed and went back to the business of war. And there is no punchline.

19 Goodwill to all men
Brits and Germans play football in No Man's Land

After four months of muddy, bloody warfare, the last thing you expect to see is the enemy putting up Christmas trees decorated with candles by their trenches!

At first, British soldiers at the Ypres Salient front thought it was a trick, but it was Christmas Eve 1914 and soon they realised their German foes were simply up for a Yuletide celebration.

Eventually, the two sides set aside their weapons and shook hands in No Man's Land. Thus began an amazing unofficial truce that lasted for several days (to the dismay of commanding officers).

The Brits soon discovered they shared a common love with our previously hated enemy: football. A member of the Bedfordshire regiment produced a ball and soldiers from both sides had a kickabout that became the stuff of legend. Mind you, no-one has ever owned up to the errant game-ending pass that saw the ball deflate on barbed wire!

Sale of the century!

In October 1919, Leeds City players were auctioned off as the club was expelled from the league for irregular payments...

LEEDS CITY PLAYER AUCTION

Hotel Metropole, Leeds
Auctioneer: Mr P Ridsdale

Lot 1
P Robinson
Athletic and agile young goalkeeper, capable of match-turning saves. Strong long-term international prospects. Likes ferrets.

Reserve price: £750

Lot 2
I Harte
Free-kick specialist with a sweet left foot. A defender whose defensive play has a lot of room for improvement. Addicted to Werthers Originals.

Reserve price: £500

Lot 3
J Morris
Short midfielder. Prone to off-field trouble. You'd be mad to buy him. But we did.

Reserve price: £23

Lot 4
D Batty
Experienced and trustworthy midfielder. So old he plays in carpet slippers, but leads by example. Do not let him take a penalty. Ever.

Reserve price: £300

EVERYONE MUST GO!

Lot 5
H Kewell
Gifted dribbler with a penchant for humiliating opposing defenders and scoring spectacular goals.

Reserve price: £1,250
(but we will accept a ridiculously low offer)

Lot 6
S Johnson
Midfielder. Average passer, average tackler, average dribbler. Really average. Hugely overpriced.

Reserve price: £5,000

Lot 7
A Smith
Fiery young centre-forward who actually cared whether Leeds City won or lost. Deserves better than to be stuck with this shower. Doesn't score many goals. Purple lips.

Reserve price: £1,200

Lot 8
M Viduka
Suspiciously fat-looking centre-forward, but lethal when he can be bothered. Which isn't often. A really bad timekeeper.

Reserve price: A$1,100

Mountie to the rescue

How PC Scorey and his shiny white horse saved the 1923 FA Cup final. In his own plodding words...

POLICE REPORT

Name	PC Scorey
Date	Saturday May 1923
Incident	Overcrowding in Wembley area

I mounted my horse Billy and proceeded to trot around the vicinity of Wembley whereupon it came to our attention that a large gathering of people had gathered. Preliminary enquiries revealed they were there to witness the final game in an Association Football competition called the Football Association Challenge Cup to be contested by clubs named Bolton Wanderers and West Ham United.

The venue for this match was Wembley Stadium, the building of which had been completed just four days previously.

The British Empire Exhibition authorities who organised the aforementioned match have since recorded an official attendance of 126,047. However, I witnessed thousands more scaling the perimeter walls and entering the ground without authorisation. My own head count would suggest that approximately 247,352 people entered the stadium.

With the assistance of other mounted officers and the cooperation of the general public, we proceeded to clear the pitch so the game could commence. Bolton won 2-0.

I had kippers for supper.

Offside! Or is it... ?

One-word rule alteration causes goal glut

In 1925, a rule change of one-word proportions occurred that shook the football world to its very proportions!

Since the Great War, the beautiful game had been blighted by dullards like Newcastle United who started playing an "offside trap". An attacking player had to have at least three – count 'em, three – opposing players between him and the goal when the ball was played to him, so it was easy to catch them out. It was like watching Arsenal under George Graham – it was that bad.

When the word "three" was changed to "two" in the rule, more goals were scored literally overnight as defenders cluelessly blundered about. 6,373 goals were scored in the Football League in 1925/26, up from 4,700 in 1924/25.

Goal-mongous!

"Oh, darling, I still don't understand that dashed offside law."

Mighty atom strikes!
Pocket-sized Patsy somersaults to glory

The 1925 Scottish Cup final between Celtic and Dundee will forever be remembered for Celtic star Patsy "The Mighty Atom" Gallagher's wonder goal.

With Dundee leading 1–0 and just 15 minutes to go, "Mighty Atom" fizzed and whirled into a crowded penalty area with the ball at his feet. Just a few feet and inches from goal, a crunching tackle stopped him in his fizzy tracks. But the Cadbury's Miniature-sized shooting star atomic creature would not be denied, somehow keeping the ball lodged between his feet and somersaulting into the net with it.

Inspired by pocket Patsy's acrobatics, Celtic went on to win 2–1 and chalk up a record 11th Scottish Cup win. Atomic Kitten!

Hip to be square

The first radio broadcast of a match...
and a new phrase is born!

1

Back in the day when televised matches and no-one playing on a Saturday afternoon any more was still just a twinkle in Rupert Murdoch's eye...

4

7

2

5

...someone came up with the bright idea of broadcasting the commentary from a football match on the radio (or wireless, as it might have still been called then)...

8

3

6

...The first game chosen for this experiment was a match between Arsenal and Sheffield United on 22 January 1927. However, broadcasters were worried...

9

10

...that listeners wouldn't be able to follow the action. So the *Radio Times* (back when its name made more sense) printed a diagram of a pitch divided into numbered squares...

13

11

...One commentator would then describe the action while another called out the number of the square so listeners would know where the action was taking place...

14

12

15

...and that's where the phrase "Back to square one" comes from! Now wasn't that educational?

25 Dai-day at Wembley

Welsh team win FA Cup!

They were singing atop Snowdon and baking Welsh cakes in the valleys (possibly) after Cardiff City beat Arsenal 1–0 in the 1927 FA Cup final. It was the, um, first time in a row that the FA Cup had been taken out of England and the Taffy invaders were jubilant.

Ironically, the winning goal for Cardiff was scored by Scottish-sounding Hughie Ferguson and conceded by Arsenal's Welsh-sounding Welsh international keeper Dan Lewis. Lewis let Fergie's weak shot spill out of his hands and over the line and Welsh football history would never be the same again. Because now it was different!

The joy of six-ty

Dixie Dean goes goal ker-azy

Who ever looked after the record books in the 1920s must have used an awful lot of sticky tape. A year after George Camsell had torn up the goalscoring stats, Everton's Dixie Dean shredded them again in the 1927/28 season when he overhauled Camsell's 59 league goals in a campaign by going one better and hitting sixty. He left it late though, needing a hat-trick from his final match. After hitting two in the first half against Arsenal, he had to wait until eight minutes from time to get the decisive 60th – a far post header. "Trixie Dixie gets to sixty" said the headlines next day. We reckon.

Achtung Zeppelin!

FA Cup final interrupted by surprise appearance of German airship

The 1930 FA Cup final could have been remembered as the day the formerly-inspired-by-Herbert-Chapman Huddersfield were beaten by the now-inspired-by-Herbert-Chapman Arsenal, who went on to dominate British football for a decade. It could also have remembered as the day the Cup saw one of it's cleverest goals – a snappily taken one-two free kick between Alex James and Cliff Bastin. But it isn't. No, it's remembered as the day a bloody great Graf Zeppelin floated over the Twin Towers in the middle of a match. A portent of things to come midway between two wars, spectators didn't know whether to boo or cheer. Reports that the Zep flew off when the Germans realised it was "ze boring, boring Arsenal playing" cannot be confirmed…

In 1930, Uruguay hosted (and won) the first World Cup. England, in their wisdom, didn't attend. ("It'll never catch on…").

However the United States team, which largely comprised former Scottish and English professionals, did reach a semi-final against Argentina. During which, an over-excited US medic tried to complain to the referee about something (possibly his side being 6–1 down) and accidentally broke a bottle of chloroform. The poor chap was overcome by the fumes and had to be stretchered off. The victorious Uruguayans presumably thought the whole event was a gas…

Your number's up...
Numbered shirts make their debut

The 1932/33 FA Cup campaign has two claims to fame. The second of which is that it ended with the first final where numbered shirts were worn: Everton wore one (their goalkeeper) to 11, and Manchester City sported 12 to 22 (their goalkeeper).

Everton emerged victorious (and presumably happy and glorious) after goals from Stein, Dunn and that man Dixie Dean again. It gave the Merseysiders a hat-trick of success: the Second Division crown in 1931, the First Division title in 1932 and now the FA Cup...

…but long after the final, people were still talking about the third round and Third Division fodder Walsall's astonishing 2–0 victory over the footballing "royalty" that was Arsenal. The match was built up as the Bank of England team (the Arsenal side had cost some £30,000) versus the little team that cost £69.

After a brutal smash and grab, however (five Walsall players could have been sent off in the first 15 minutes, such was their, ahem, committed style of play) the Bank of England had been well and truly robbed.

The 1938 FA Cup final between Preston and Huddersfield had been a fairly drab affair until the final few seconds of extra time. With the score 0–0 and a goal never looking to be on the cards, BBC radio commentator Tom Woodroofe even promised listeners: "If they score now I'll eat my hat." Uh-oh Tom.

Approximately one second after his utterance, Preston's George Mutch was tackled just outside the box. Except, in these pre-Specsavers days, the referee decided it was just inside the box and awarded a penalty.

Mutch, who'd been knocked out by the challenge admitted afterwards: "I didn't even understand that a penalty had been awarded. They handed me the ball and I placed it automatically. As I took my run-up I wondered what I was doing and why. I don't remember aiming at the goal."

He was so groggy, he almost missed, but the ball just bounced over the line after coming off the crossbar.

Tom bought a new hat...

Win or die!
War looms as Mussolini, erm, encourages Italy to
World Cup victory

The year 1938 wasn't the happiest. Spain was in the throes of Civil War,
Musolini's Italy had invaded Abyssinia and Hitler's Germany had annexed
Austria. This was the background to the World Cup finals in France (to
be the last finals for a dozen years). Italy went on to win the tournament
after rumours that Mussolini had sent them a threatening telegram on
matchday. Quite unbelievably, we have managed to obtain that telegram…

Indicazione d'urgenza

Circuito sul quale si deve fare
l'inoltro del telegramma

Ufficio Telegrafico di ROMA
T E L E G R A M M A

```
***CIAO EVERYBODY STOP HOPE YOU ARE WELL STOP
I'M FINE STOP WEATHER IS GOOD STOP I CAN SEE
THE CAMPAIGN HERE IN ABYSSINIA IS GOING WELL
FROM MY HOTEL ROOM STOP GOOD LUCK IN THE FINAL
STOP WIN OR DIE STOP LOVE AND KISSES M
```

The world at war

The season comes to a premature end

On 2 September 1939, Blackpool were top of the First Division, the only team with maximum points. Just below them were Arsenal, who'd just beaten Sunderland 5–2, with Ted Drake scoring four. It was shaping up to be an exciting campaign. But there would in fact be no more league football for seven seasons.

"Maximum points, top of the league, this is our yea... oh bugger."

33 Both sides now

Stan's the man... for the hosts and the visitors

In an unusual display of sportsmanship, on 25 September 1943 at Wembley, England allowed their twelfth man Stan Mortensen to go on as a sub for Wales as the visitors had no spare players after Ivor Powell got injured. Perhaps the generosity was a sign of confidence from the hosts. If so, it was justified as England ran out 8–3 winners. Now if England could just get Wales to return the favour with Ryan Giggs...

34 Sunderland slope off
Giant killers Yeovil upset the odds again

After beating Second Division Bury in the third round of the 1948/49 FA Cup, giant killers Yeovil from the Southern League added the First Division scalp of mighty Sunderland in the fourth round. The Somerset club and their infamous sloping pitch played host to the visitors from the North-East with few expecting anything but a Sunderland victory. And when Yeovil's keeper was hurt in training and had to be replaced by solicitor's clerk Dickie Dyke (one previous senior appearance) the astronomical odds against them increased by the size of several planets (roughly).

10 minutes into the match, Yeovil's winger Hargreaves pulled a muscle, becoming a virtual passenger for the rest of the game. By now the odds were scientifically proven to be too large to calculate on any known calculator.

The only player in the Yeovil team with any League experience was their player-manager Alec Stock, who described his two roles as "violent exercise on top of a pile of worries". Although it was Sunderland who were worrying after Stock smacked in a goal from the edge of the box. They were a bit less worried when Robinson got them an equaliser but even more worried than they had been before when in extra time Bryant put Yeovil back in the lead. And then the ref blew the final whistle and Sunderland weren't worried any more. They were just sad.

American strife
England humiliated in the World Cup by the USA

Despite being joint favourites, with Brazil, going into the 1950 World Cup finals, England (yes, we'd finally agreed to participate in the thing) were embarrassed by a 1–0 defeat by the United States and the players would have come home with their tails between their legs if they'd had tails.

Neither they nor the English press pack stayed on to watch the deciding match in which Brazil lost to Uruguay before 199,854 fans.

However, American disinterest in the sport meant the victory over England barely merited any column inches at all. As this, ahem, authentic cutting from the time illustrates…

Wizard of the dribble
The Stanley Matthews Cup final

Back in 1953, the world's most famous footballer didn't wear sarongs, change his hairstyle every five minutes or have a pop star wife. But despite not bringing out an autobiography every Christmas, Stanley Matthews (yes, that's who we're talking about) was incredibly popular. So popular in fact that come the Cup final that year the whole country were willing him and the rest of the Blackpool team on. Well, apart from Bolton fans, who presumably wanted their

Matthews starts here...

team to win. With two previous Cup outings ending in failure, many believed this was Stanley's last chance for a medal. And with 55 minutes gone, it wasn't looking too good: Bolton were 3–1 up. Yikes! Fortunately, an irresistible Matthews led the recovery with a series of superb runs down the wing, inspiring Blackpool to an epic recovery and 4–3 win.

A nation rejoiced and Stanley didn't even feel the need to write a book about it. Hooray!

... and finishes here!

Home truths

England get a lesson in modern football at Wembley

It had always been assumed, well by the English anyway, that the best nation in the world at football were… well, England of course. But on a brisk November afternoon at Wembley in 1953 Hungary's "Magic Magyars" put paid to such thoughts. Not only did they inflict England's first home defeat by continental opposition, they ran riot, demolishing the hosts 6–3 and putting paid to any lingering thoughts of superiority with their vastly more polished display.

The Times summed up the mood of the nation when it reported: "Yesterday, the inevitable happened. England at last were beaten by the foreign invader." Ouch.

Injury time

Cup final keeper plays on with a broken neck

People handle pain in different ways. Some are hysterical, some bravely stoic. And some, like Bert Trautmann, are completely bloody oblivious to it. The Manchester City goalkeeper was playing in the 1956 FA Cup final when, with 15 minutes left, he dived at the feet of Birmingham's Peter Murphy. He got up, dazed and reeling, but to the crowd's chorus of "For he's a jolly good fellow," carried on playing as his side won 3–1.

Three days later, after complaining of "headaches", x-rays revealed he had in fact broken his neck and one too-firm pat on the back could have killed him. Safe to say from then on no-one ever accused Bert of being a drama queen…

"Now Mr Trautmann, let's have a look at you… Argh!"

The beautiful game

Brazil rule and Pele becomes a household name

Edson Arantes do Nascimento was only 17 when he came to the World Cup finals in Sweden in the summer of 1958. He made his debut in Brazil's third qualifying game, against the Soviet Union. Three matches and six Pele goals later, Brazil were world champions and Pele was a household name.

The Brazilians were simply in a different class to Europe's finest, whom they made look more pedestrian than a zebra crossing full of penguins (or something), with better tactics and unbelievable skills. There was a new football world order and Brazil were, very clearly, at the top of it.

"If only we could sell personalised replica shirts, we'd make a fortune."

You win the greatest club cup competition in the world; you collect the famous FA Cup from a royal dignitary; you parade around the pitch in front of cheering fans doing silly dances and taking turns to put the trophy lid on your head… it's every footballer's dream. But in 1960, victorious Wolves players had to use the famous trophy as a shield as angry Blackburn Rovers fans pelted them with apple cores and orange peel (they didn't have frankfurters and M&Ms back in the olden days).

The match had been totally rubbish and hinged on an unlucky injury to Blackburn left-back Dave Whelan, who broke his leg trying to tackle Wolves' Norman Deeley after half an hour when the score was just 1–0 to Wolves.

As no substitutes were yet allowed 10-man Rovers succumbed to a 3–0 defeat, with Deeley scoring twice in the second-half using his unbroken legs. Frustrated by the Wolves players' fierce tackling and the inaction of Kevin Howley (the youngest man to referee a Cup final) Rovers fans threw rubbish during the traditional lap of honour causing the media to dub the shame game the "Dustbin Final".

Footie on the box

The League dabble with TV... well, it was the Sixties

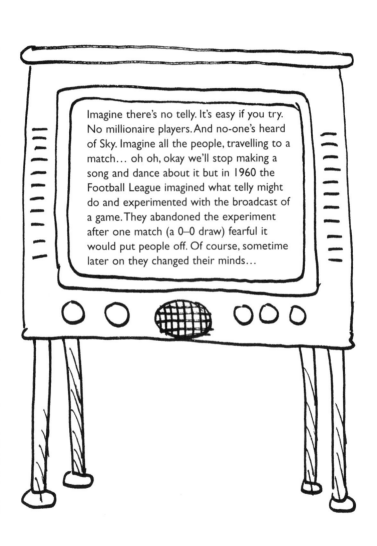

Imagine there's no telly. It's easy if you try. No millionaire players. And no-one's heard of Sky. Imagine all the people, travelling to a match... oh oh, okay we'll stop making a song and dance about it but in 1960 the Football League imagined what telly might do and experimented with the broadcast of a game. They abandoned the experiment after one match (a 0–0 draw) fearful it would put people off. Of course, sometime later on they changed their minds...

Player power, 'eh? Long before England players were allegedly threatening to strike over drug test shenanigans there was an even bigger threat of strike action.

In 1961, players were getting tired of the deal surrounding their wages and contracts. They were restricted to a maximum salary of £20 – far less than they could earn abroad. And they weren't allowed to move to a club of their choosing when their contract expired. A "slave contract" Jimmy Hill called it.

Yes, he of the remarkable chinnage was the chairman of the Professional Footballers Association at the time and threatened to bring his members out on strike if changes weren't forthcoming.

When the strike was called for January 21, the League insisted all clubs move their games to the 20th to avoid it. "What a way to run a sport," jeered the *Daily Mirror* in an editorial entitled "Idiotic!"

Fortunately, the League backed down and Chinny prevailed. Football had been dragged out of the dark ages and there would never be any rows again... (What's that? Oh, okay scrap that last bit).

48 Lawman swamped
Denis Law's six-goal haul is washed out

The 1960/61 FA Cup fourth round tie between Manchester City and Luton Town at Kenilworth Road turned into Swan Lake with boots (sort of) as torrential rain reduced the pitch to a mushy-pea-like bog. Luton squelched into a 2–0 lead within 15 minutes before balletic City striker Denis Law proved he could walk, dribble and score on water!

While all around him sloshed and slithered, twinkle-toes Law fired in six goals. But with City 6–2 up and 21 minutes remaining, the referee must have decided his socks were getting a little *too* uncomfortably wet and abandoned the game. In the rematch, luckless Law scored again but City were sunk 3–1 by the lucky Luton.

"Och, c'mon, ref, It's still playable"

44 Stan's pulling power
Matthews makes triumphant return to Stoke

Some players simply put bums on seats (er, or at least, feet on terraces). Stanley Matthews was such a player. In 1961, when the 46-year-old Matthews returned to Stoke City after a 14-year absence (he'd been playing for Blackpool), the club attendance shot up from 8,000 to 35,000 in the space of one game. Which made his Stoke team-mates particularly happy – they received a bonus of £1 for every thousand fans attending over the 12,000 mark.

After just a few unhappy months spent in Italy, Jimmy Greaves returned to British football in December 1961 for a record transfer fee when Tottenham spent £99,999 to buy him from Milan. The Spurs manager Bill Nicholson deliberately made the fee one pound short of six figures because he didn't want Greaves to feel pressurised by being the first £100,000 footballer.

The striker certainly didn't seem too stressed – he scored a hat-trick on his debut.

HALF-TIME

46 The big chill
Flamin' hell, it was freezing!

It was cold, the winter of 1962/63. So cold that even more football matches than normal were postponed. In fact, after Christmas the football authorities were starting to get really rather worried. On 5 January, only three of the 32 FA Cup third round matches could take place and just a handful of league games. The following week it was even worse with only eight matches in the country going ahead. Soon, some matches had been delayed and re-arranged more than 10 times.

Eventually, the season had to be extended by several weeks. But not before clubs had tried some bizarre solutions to beat the freeze. Leicester put a tent over their pitch, but Blackpool went the furthest – employing a flame thrower in the vain hope of softening up their pitch.

It didn't work but we suspect there must be a "the season was really hotting up" gag in there somewhere…

The price of glory
Can money really buy the title?

Blue shirts, cheque book at the ready. No not the current set-up at Chelsea. This was back in those more "innocent" times, the sixties. Although perhaps it was only the prices that differed. Having spent £175,000 on new players the previous season, Everton proceeded to pay another £100,000 on a couple more to make a challenge for the 1963 League championship. It paid off as the Merseysiders cruised to the title although critics labelled them "cheque book champions". The celebrating Evertonians didn't seem too upset though...

48 The twelfth man
League finally allows substitutes

After years of ten-man sides, the League finally decided that from the start of the 1965/66 season, teams would be allowed to have one substitute on the bench who could come on in replacement of an injured player. Which, given some of the, ahem, challenges that still passed for tackles, was probably a good idea.

"He says it was his own number 12 who kicked him…"

What's the difference?
A tale of broken Hearts

Sometimes, it's the little things that matter. Like goal difference. Or goal average as it was back in 1965. (Now, stick with us because this next bit is complicated).

On the final day of the Scottish season, Kilmarnock beat Hearts 2–0. This meant both clubs had played 34 games, won 22, drawn six and lost six. But Hearts had scored 90 and conceded 49 goals, whilst Kilmarnock had scored 62 and conceded 33. On goal *average* (remember, that was the method of the day) that made Kilmarnock champions, and so they were. But

a bitterly disappointed Hearts pointed out that if matters had been settled on goal *difference*, they would have won the title.

Hearts demanded the rules were changed, and the League agreed – from the following season. Which wasn't much consolation to Hearts fans.

As a somewhat ironic postscript, some 21 years later Hearts were pipped to the title by Celtic – on goal difference. If the old method of goal average had still applied, it would have been Hearts instead who were champions. Doh!

Viva El Beatle!
Bestie gets the Fab Four treatment

Isn't Georgie Best just the fabbest?!
Those crazy Benfica fans certainly think
so. They got hip to him the moment he
took a stroll through their pad in 1966
with his mop top and his rubber soles
and scored two goals in 12 minutes.
Georgie and his Manchester United mates
ended up 5-1 winners and Benfica were
no longer toppermost of the poppermost.
After the game, Georgie was mobbed to
cries of "El Beatle" and one fan even tried
to cut off a lock of his hair. Georgie took it
all in his stride and flew back to Blighty
with a smile like a sunbeam and wearing
a sombrero. Why the hip hat GB?
"I dunno, I just wanted a souvenir," says
Georgie Boy. Far out!

Stop! Thief! Woof!

Dog gets the FA out of a pickle

It's not really what you want is it? A few months before you're about to host the World Cup and suddenly the trophy goes missing.

The FA was suitably embarrassed when it transpired that the Jules Rimet trophy, left in Central Hall, Westminister, had been stolen. The thief didn't take the stamps that were also in the hall. A shame for him as they were worth some £3million (the World Cup was only worth about £3,000).

The thief was never caught but the trophy was discovered a week later by a dog named Pickles in some bushes in Norwood, south London. Although, thinking about it, it was probably his owner who phoned the authorities.

Champions of the world

England's wingless wonders come good

The 1966 World Cup final. And one question remains unanswered: Did it cross the line? The Germans said "No", we said, "Yea… ooh!" and Backhramov the Russian linesman said "Yes" (hey, we were going to say yes too, we were just thinking about it first, that's all, honest).

All that matters is that Geoff Hurst's second goal, and England's third, counted.

Even before that drama there had already been plenty of thrills (and, hey, maybe even some spills). West Germany took the lead after 12 minutes through Haller. Hurst equalised six minutes later. England gained the advantage in the 78th minute after Peters struck home and then Germany heart-breakingly got a late equaliser through Weber seconds before the whistle.

Extra time could have gone either way. "You've beaten them once, now do it again" was Alf Ramsey's advice. "Look at them, they're finished!" (He wasn't a man of many words, Alf).

Alan Ball found some extra pace in his tired legs, crossed the ball to Hurst who turned and smashed it against the underside of the bar and down onto the line… but did it cross that line?

The record books say yes and Hurst put the result beyond doubt in the final seconds. Blimey, England had won the World Cup!

Jock's bhoys quad joy!

Jock Stein's Celtic do the Quadruple!

There was a day when a Scottish team stood astride European football like a really big colossus. That day was the 1966/67 season, and that team was Celtic, and that Celtic was managed by Jock Stein.

After winning all three domestic competitions, Jock's team of Bhoys headed for Lisbon to try and become the first British team ever to win the European Cup.

The apocryphal script for the final said that classy opponents Inter Milan would finally expose the, well, crapness, of Scottish football. But canny Jock took that Italian script and wrote another more Scottish one.

He made sure his players were so relaxed they were singing songs in the tunnel before the game, which, like, totally freaked out the Italians.

Then big Jock upstaged the great Inter coach Helenio Herrera by sitting on the bench Herrera had earmarked for himself, and refusing to budge.

What remained of that original script was completely shredded when goals by Tommy Gemmell and Steve Chalmers gave Celtic a 2–1 win. The Bhoys had won the Quad!

Sealed with a (Millwall) kiss

Wolf man KO'd by 'Wall man

There's nothing like the thrill of a last-minute goal to spark a joyous pitch invasion. And when Wolves striking legend Derek Dougan scored a last-gasp equaliser in a Second Division match against Millwall in April 1967, it was nothing like a joyous pitch invasion.

Happy Wolf "The Doog" turned to celebrate with a supporter who'd run on the pitch, only belatedly to deduce that it was an angry Millwall fan. The clue was probably in the fact that the fan punched him in the face...

55 Don't walk!

New ruling forces keepers to keep in step

Season 1967/68 was a sad one for guardians of the onion bag as the International Football Board introduced a new rule limiting goalkeepers to four steps while holding the ball before releasing it into play. Thus spectators were denied the thrilling spectacle of goalies zig-zagging across their penalty area trampling on valuable grass and chewing up seconds of essential playing time.

A goalkeeper we would have spoken to at the time if we hadn't just made him up was outraged: "It's an absolute infringement of my human rights. Some of my happiest minutes are spent carrying a ball round the penalty area while opposition centre-forwards try to kick me up the arse." Strangely, no-one listened.

Pat sticks one in the onion bag
Shot-stopper shoots and scores in Charity Shield thriller

Traditionally, Charity Shield matches are dishwater dull, but one mighty punt by Tottenham Hotspur keeper Pat Jennings added Fairy Liquid froth to the 1967 game, a 3–3 thriller between Spurs and Manchester United at Old Trafford.

Big Pat, whose shovel-like hands made a football look like a ping-pong ball showed he also had big feet when he sent a huge kick upfield from the edge of the Spurs penalty area.

A high wind (and perchance a little puff from Mother Nature?) sent the ball swirling over Spurs forwards and United defenders, before bouncing over the tortured head of a furiously back-pedalling United keeper Alex Stepney and into the goal.

"I couldn't believe it," laughed big punter Pat afterwards. "I wasn't even sure it counted in the laws of the game."

Well Pat, it did.

The Yo-Yo club

When they were up, they were up, and when they were down, they were down...

Yo, yo, yo, YO! In 1969, Northampton Town completed a dizzying Yo-Yo ride from the Fourth Division to the First Division and back down again. Town's phoenix-like rise from the ashes began in 1960. Within five seasons they were sucking up oxygen in the highest altitudes of English football. They really sucked though, and it took them just four seasons to splash land in the heap of Fourth Division ashes from whence they had, er, hitherto risen.

Football starts war!

Fiery Honduras-El Salvador World Cup encounter ends badly

When some furry-handed Sky presenter hypes up a handbags at dawn clash between a monkey-faced, gurning Arsenal defender and an equine-headed Manchester United striker, you might think football's turned into some kind of warzone. But back in 1969, it really did! Yes, the (deep breath) World Cup Central & North American Zone qualifying group semi-final tie between El Salvador and Honduras actually sparked a full-scale war between the two countries.

The two-legged tie was level after two legs, so they had to play a decider. Crowd riots at all three games provoked running battles along the Honduras–El Salvador border. El Salvador finally prevailed 3–2 in the deciding game.

Rather than exchange the traditional polite end-of-game handshakes, the two countries opted instead to break off diplomatic relations. A fortnight later El Salvador invaded Honduras. It was war!

In the summer of 1970, UEFA decreed that matches that finished all-square in their European competitions would no longer be decided by the toss of a coin, but by the test of nerve and skill that is the penalty shoot-out.

On 3 September 1970, Gareth Southgate was born.

Simply Brazilliant!

Fans go nuts about 1970 World Champs

Clodoaldo, Tostao, Rivelino, Jairzinho, Pele-o... the names of Brazil's 1970 World Cup-winning stars slip off the tongue as smoothly as Castrol GTX (kids, don't try that at home).

Brazil steamrollered dullards Italy 4–1 in the final in Mexico City, but the *real* final was their group match against the mighty Three Lions in Guadalajara: Banksie's save from Pele (flip reversed in mid-air, wasn't it?), Jairzinho's winning goal (Tostao beats three, passes to Pele, pops it to Jairzinho and it's a goooooooooaaaalllll!), Jeff Astle's infamous miss (ooh!), Mooro and Pele exchanging shirts at the end (aah!)... it was the beautiful game at it's Brazil-nuts-for goalposts most beautiful. Marvellous.

Mooro thunderbolt KOs ref!

West Ham and England legend blows whistle on groggy ref

Bobby Moore: a name synonymous with sportsmanship, dignity and all that is good about English football. Born with an innate ability to read the game, Mooro was always a couple of yards ahead of the average footballer in his head and on grass… even when he was knocking out referees!

During a game for West Ham v Wolves on 14 November 1970, Mooro's thunderous clearance scored a direct hit on the man in black, knocking him unconscious. Quick-thinking Bobby, who'd scored a great goal earlier in the match, immediately grabbed the prostrate ref's whistle, blew it to stop the game and called for the physio. What a man, what a mighty, mighty good man.

In 1973/74, midweek matches were suspended because of power cuts caused by the miner's strike. And as winter approached, clubs were allowed to kick off their Saturday games at 2.15pm so they finished before sunset.

Bizarrely, it was felt that powering floodlights for our glorious national game was a lower priority than heating homes or boiling an egg. Bizarre…

If only the Football Association had listened to our bright idea to invite all striking miners to watch evening games for free, they could have used their helmet lamps to illuminate the pitch. Simple.

Arm-breaker Luigi's leg broken
Ledge Luigi gets his leguppance

Between 1965 and 1974, Italian striking legend Luigi Riva bashed in a record 35 goals in 42 internationals. Renowned for his speed, courage and deadly left-foot shot, Luigi was one of Italy's best-loved players. One fan didn't love Luigi quite so much though after Luigi unleashed one of his deadly accurate shots, missed the goal by a mile and broke the fan's arm during a practice match in October 1970.

But by a bone-shattering crunch of fate, a few days later, Italy played Austria in Vienna and deadly legend Luigi was stretchered off with a broken leg. Snap!

64 "The Chin" saves the day: Part 2

It's that man again!

You just can't keep a good man with a protuberant chin and funny beard down! Having freed footballers from slavery back in 1961 (see moment 42), Chinny saved civilisation yet again during a match between Liverpool and Arsenal at Highbury in September 1972. When a linesman got injured, "Sir" Jimmy (Saville's got a knighthood, so why no gong for Hill, eh Mr Prime Minister?) temporarily abandoned his commentator's microphone and took up the official's flag. Clearly, he was unsuited to a job that traditionally attracts know-all busy-bodies who love the sound of their own voice, but Jimmy took it all on the chin.

Clown makes fool of England

Circus entertainer tames Three Lions in one night!

All that stood between England and the 1974 World Cup finals was a circus entertainer! Before England's final qualifying match against Poland, which England needed to win, outspoken Derby manager and TV pundit Brian Clough informed the nation that the Polish goalkeeper Jan Tomaszewski was a clown.

For someone more used to slinging custard pies and squirting water out of plastic flowers, Jan proved to be a pretty handy keeper. Clearly, his training as a physical comedian stood him in good stead as he used every part of his anatomy – fist, fingertip, leg, hand, torso, wig – to repel shot after shot. He was beaten just once, by an Allan Clarke penalty, but the game finished 1–1 and England were eliminated.

Soon goalkeepers up and down the country were training in big red plastic shoes. Possibly.

The best World Cups are when a team or a player does something so innovative or brilliant that every kid in the world immediately wants to repeat the trick in the playground. Which makes the 1974 World Cup a particularly fine event.

Two teams dominated. Germany, with their revolutionary sweeper system, that was sort of like the Italians but with the sweeper (the legendary Beckenbauer) starting attacks rather than just mopping up at the back. And Holland, whose equally revolutionary "Total Football" (everyone can play everywhere, orchestrated by the also-legendary Cruyff) was simply very, very exciting to watch.

In the final, Germany came out on top but Cruyff at least has the knowledge that every single kid in the world spent the next few years tying themselves in knots trying to master the Cruyff turn.

"Aarggh, mum!"

67 X-Rated action

Crackpot coppers recommend film-style match classifications

Football hooliganism. It's not big and it's not clever. Although neither were the bright sparks at the Police Superintendents Association.

During the 1975/76 season they suggested one way to combat the growing hooliganism problem was by "rating" matches with a film-style classification. That way, people would know what to expect when they went to a game. (No, really!)

Funnily enough, the idea didn't catch on. But if it had done, and if there had been a police officer could Jonathan Woss, and if he wrote film-style previews of matches, who knows what it might have looked like...

Whether you're a fighter or a family

WOSSY'S FAMILY FAVOURITE

Isle Of Skye v Isle of Eigg

Fancy a local derby without the aggro this weekend? Then why not make the short trip to the north-west of Scotland, hop on a ferry to the Isle of Eigg and witness this clash of the titans. Mix freely with opposition fans and chat to the island's one policeman. Not many people live on Eigg so if there's injuries you might even get a game! The queue for Bovril at half-time moves fast and your kids will love the 5p sausage rolls (home-made by Mrs Auchterlogie). The football will be crap.
Wossy's rating: U

RATINGS: XXX - Bring a gun X - Extreme violence. No

WOSSY AT THE FOOTIE

Leeds v Manchester United

Definitely not for the kids, but hard-core hoolies will relish this one. Knuckledusters, knives, machetes, samurai swords and rifles are often carried at this fixture... and that's just by the police. Beware of flying bricks and replica Jocky Wilson darts. Sew up jacket pockets to deter predatory urinators.

Wossy's rating: X

Liverpool v Everton

Scousers only - anyone who doesn't find Liverpool's "legendary Scouse wit" funny should give Anfield a wide berth. Red-Blue family feuds may escalate into full-scale slanging matches. And beware: Cilla Black has been booked to sing "You'll Never Walk Alone" at half-time!

Wossy's rating: 12

Leicester City v Derby County

Always an incendiary fixture, but undercover cop PC McIntyre (photo available on request) has infiltrated Leicester City's notorious Walkers Crispy gang and his intelligence should ensure the match goes off without going off big-style. Avoid large groups of socially-inadequate, middle-aged, shaven-headed men who smell of cheeseburgers and hand grenades.

Wossy's rating: X

Millwall v Whoever they are playing

Do not go within five miles of this match. Seriously, don't. You will die.

Wossy's rating: XXX

FA block FA kissing ban move
Goalscorers given all-clear to get jiggy widdit

In 1975/76, the Football Association's Match Committee suggested players who "kissed and cuddled" after a goal was scored should be charged with bringing the game into disrepute.

Favouring a stiff handshake themselves, the uptight old codgers wanted to deny fans the chance to see their heroes writhing in post-goal ecstasy. Happily, other members of the FA more comfortable with their sexuality rejected the proposal as "impracticable", and players remained free to express their beautiful love any which way they pleased.

Fourth Division Watford got a rocket man-powered boost in May 1976 when multi-millionaire glam rock star and alleged astronaut Elton John became their new chairman.

"I'm really serious about this, I hope people will not treat this as a gimmick," Mr John told the assembled press as he adjusted his star-shaped spectacles and eased his platform boots under the boardroom table.

70 Revie sheiks on Dubai deal
England boss deserts to the desert

In July '77, dastardly England boss Don Revie shocked the nation when he defected to the desert. After winning just 14 and losing seven out of 29 internationals in three years, and with England needing a miracle to qualify for the 1978 World Cup finals, Don jumped before he was pushed.

Before formally resigning, crafty Don privately spoke to the FA and generously offered to "save trouble and go" if they paid up the rest of his contract (£50,000).

When asked if he had another job lined up, absent-mined Don said "No", forgetting that he'd already negotiated a £340,000 tax-free four-year contract to manage the United Arab Emirates. It seems that, previously, instead of going to Helsinki to scout future World Cup qualifying opponents Italy against Finland, Don had accidentally got on a plane to Dubai instead. As you do.

After old dastard Don walked off into the golden tax-free sunset, fans expected the FA to appoint a safe, uncontroversial figure to steady the ship. Surprisingly though, they didn't give Don's old job to Brian Clough, opting instead for outspoken maverick Ron Greenwood.

Double-sided Pele says farewell
Brazilian ledge swaps teams in final match!

On 1 October 1977, arguably the greatest player of all-time (apart from Maradona and John Fashanu) and the future face of Viagra, ended his 22-year career with a farewell exhibition match between Brazilian club Santos and New York Cosmos. Pele had scored 1,090 goals in 1,114 games for Santos before retiring in 1974 and then unretiring to play for the Cosmos.

77,000 people packed the 77,000-capacity Giants Stadium to see the future credit card salesman play the first half for New York Cosmos (scoring a stunning free-kick) and the second half wearing the Santos number 10 shirt he'd made famous.

If only Pele had swapped his Santos, Cosmos or Brazil shirts for an England shirt and been English throughout his career, English football history would have been very much better indeed.

"Don't worry, he's playing for your lot in the second half."

Hordes of tartan-clad loons celebrated Scotland 2–1 Home Championship-clinching win over England in 1977 with a boozy pitch invasion. The victory took their tally of wins over the Auld Enemy on English soil to a massive five since 1938, and understandably the sozzled Scots fans wanted soiled souvenirs of the occasion.

The merry mentalists gleefully set about digging up sods of turf until the goalmouths were bereft of sods, as well as cracking both crossbars and tearing down the goal nets. A total of 132 haggis-munching Wembley wreckers were arrested that weekend and £18,000 of damage was caused, but a few living rooms in Scotland would soon display their own little piece of England...

73 Britain's first million quid player!

Cloughie shoves all his chips on a guy called Trevor

Nowadays, a million pounds might buy you Seth Johnson's left calf muscle, but in the Seventies you could buy three whole good players for that amount. That was until 9 February 1979 when Nottingham Forest boss Brian Clough decided to spend £1,180,000 on just one player: Birmingham City and England striker Trevor Francis. Thus a man named Trevor became Britain's first million pound player, smashing the previous transfer fee record of £500,000.

The, um, striking disadvantage of buying a striker so late in the season was that Francis would only be eligible for one match in the European Cup – the final.

Cloughie had not just put all his chips on Francis, he'd smothered them in ketchup. But his gamble paid off, because Forest made the final, Francis played and scored the winner. Pontoon!

Fergie breaks old firm duopoly
Minnows monopolise 1979/80 Scottish Championship

In the game of Duopoly that is Scottish football, the Old Firm of Celtic and Rangers traditionally own all the streets, houses and hotels and rarely go directly to jail without passing "Go". But in 1979/80, long-time tenants Aberdeen managed by future knight of the realm Alex Ferguson forcibly bought up the Old Firm's Scottish League Championship hotel. It was only the second time Aberdeen had won the title in their 77-year history and first time since 1965 that neither Celtic nor Rangers had won the league. Their Duopoly board was blasted to smithereens. For a while.

75 Just like the real thing

QPR replace their pitch with artificial turf

When is grass not grass? When it's astroturf. In 1981 Queens Park Rangers decided to improve on the best that Mother Nature can offer by digging up their pitch and replacing it with an all-weather artificial surface. The club saw it as a shrewd plan that would enable Loftus Road to stage other events during the week and bring in more money to the Second Division club. But, things didn't go exactly to plan. After an initially warm response players started to complain that the ball bounced unnaturally high and that any sort of sliding contact resulted in carpet burns.

Soon, QPR realised that the grass is actually greener on the other side, especially if it's, er, grass and went back to the real thing.

"You get a nice even bounce on this pitch..."

Robert "Cap'n Bob" Maxwell, hailed as a hero for saving Oxford United, became somewhat less popular after buying a controlling interest in Reading. Especially when he revealed his plan to merge the two teams into one, called Thames Valley Royals. Oxford fans staged a sit-in on the pitch while a black coffin was paraded around Reading. Which most observers interpeted as a sign that the fans possibly weren't happy. The merger was eventually foiled. As was the Captain's later attempt (good grief) to buy Manchester United.

"Divine" Diego
The best and worst of Maradona

England were knocked out of the 1986 World Cup by eventual winners Argentina. The South Americans first goal was actually a deliberate handball by Maradona but went unpunished by what can only be described (well, by us) as short-sighted officials. TV cameras revealed the truth but Maradona shrugged off the incident, brazenly describing it as "The Hand of God".

A shell-shocked England, having witnessed the worst of Maradona, then saw the best as he waltzed embarrassingly effortlessly past almost the entire team to score a stunning solo goal. Darn.

It later transpired that God (an England fan ever since He created Saint Gary Lineker) was none too pleased to be associated with the cheating one's goal. As another of our (cough) exclusives can exclusively reveal...

The Catholic Times

June 1986

WORLD EXCLUSIVE SPECIAL

DON'T FORCE MY HAND SAYS GOD

Big boss slams Archbishop

WORLD EXCLUSIVE

God today launched a scathing attack on the Archbishop of Buenos Aires designed to scath, and attack.

In an open letter, that anyone can openly read, the number one Amighty, He-who-must-be-obeyed SLAMMED Maradona for claiming use of His hand, BLASTED the Archbishop for celebrating the goal and LAMBASTED officials for not following his instructions. The Big Cheese, currently holidaying in an exclusive hideaway with his showbiz chums Elton John and Wendy Richard, took time out from his break to pen the following missive, which was delivered on a thunderbolt to Buenos Aires Cathedral:

> Dear Bishop,
>
> Hello. How are you? I'm fine. Weather here is good. From my hotel room I have a lovely view of the beach. It's very nice (one of my better ones). Now what's this I hear that Argentinians are claiming Maradona's first goal was the, ahem "Hand of God"?
>
> I would like it publicly noted for the record that my hand was nowhere near that goal. It was here with the rest of me, getting a tan. I've never liked that Diego (apart from the "loving all mankind" thing, obviously).
>
> Why can't he use the God-given talents I gave him more appropriately. God knows what will become of him (I really do, and I can tell you - it's not pretty).
>
> Anyway, must dash. Elton's having a very glitzy barbeque and I want to get a few autographs. As I say, no more dragging me into this matter. I'm on holiday for God's sake!
>
> Best wishes
>
> G

The Crazy Gang
Wimbledon and their unique, er, spirit

The 1987/88 season showed both sides (or should that be cheeks?) of Wimbledon Football Club. The minnows from South London rose from obscurity to the top flight through a combination of luck, skill, determination, team spirit and, oh yes, kicking the ball very high in the air and running after it.

Their finest moment came in the 1988 FA Cup when they pullled off one of the biggest shocks ever by beating Liverpool 1–0 in the final. Peter Beardsley did actually score for Liverpool but the referee pulled play back for a Liverpool free kick. While the players were still disputing that Lawrie Sanchez scored for the Dons.

That season the club were also charged with bringing the game into disrepute when nine of their players dropped their shorts during a testimonial game. Bums.

PC Brian

Cloughie takes the law into his own hands

Ah, Brian Clough, so much to answer for. Including on occasion taking policing matters into his own hands. In January 1989, after Nottingham Forest's 5–2 defeat of QPR in the quarter-finals of the League Cup, some fans made the foolish decision to invade the pitch.

Cloughie was having none of it. He grabbed two fans, clipped them round the ears and dragged them off the pitch. Some hailed him a hero, others felt he shouldn't have descended to their level. Cloughie apologised, as did the fans and order was restored – apart from the fact that the FA banned the Forest manager from the touchline for the rest of the season. Spoilsports.

"Don't need to go there these days… Cloughie takes care of things!"

80 Tears of a clown
Gazza gets it off his chest at the World Cup

The 1990 World Cup, whilst an otherwise goal-lite and cynical affair was in fact one of England's best efforts. We reached the semi-finals inspired by, arguably, the player of the tournament, Paul Gascoigne.

The plastic boob-wearing, childishly simple Gascoigne could be an absolute idiot, as he was the first to admit, but on the pitch he was anything but a tit (most of the time).

Against Belgium in the second round, he earned England a quarter-final place. In the last minute of extra time he picked up a ball just outside the England penalty area and ran straight at the heart of the Belgian midfield. In their panic to stop him, the Belgians conceded a free-kick. Gascoigne grabbed the ball, launched it over the defence to the incoming David Platt who volleyed home.

A quarter-final against Cameroon subsequently successfully negotiated, meant England were now only one game from the final. Of course it did involve having to face the Germans in Turin, but still, one game away!

A 1–1 draw took the match to penalties and missses from Stuart Pearce and Chris Waddle ended England's stay.

The abiding memory, though, was not the penalty misses but the sight of a tearful Gascoigne after he picked up the booking that ensured he would have missed the final had England reached it.

The next day's newspapers, full of Gascoigne's tears, hit a nerve with the country and we welcomed him into our collective, um, bosom.

Diego hangs his shirt up
The fall and fall of Maradona

One minute you're top of the world, the next you're, well, somewhere near the scrapheap. Diego Maradona's decline came in unpleasant chunks of tabloid scandal and stupid decisions.

In 1991, he left Italy in disgrace after a drugs and sex scandal. A national opinion poll at the time found he was less popular with Italians than Saddam Hussein.

He had one more World Cup outing but was sent home from the US in disgrace after failing a drugs test. His final appearance in an Argentinian 10 was a testimonial. Afterwards the shirt was "retired" from the national team.

82 Goody two boots
Saint Lineker wins award

As he came to the end of a remarkable career in 1991 (with only a brief sojourn to Japan to come) Gary Lineker was given a Fifa Fair Play award and a cheque for £20,000 for having never been booked or sent-off in his career. He collected his prize with a shrug and a smile, as a choir of angels sang beatitudes. Slowly, Gary spread his wings and flew into the light… well the lights of a TV studio for his new career as a pundit.

83 It's a steel!
Middlesbrough carelessly lose sponsor

The cornerstone of modern football is sponsorship. All those dull and dusty corporations believe, because of their association with the beautiful game, that we'll all buy more phones, crisps, boots, cars, umbrellas, whatever. However, they expect a little something for their cash. So when British Steel discovered that the club they were funding in the 1990s, Middlesbrough, had constructed their new £16 million stadium using only 2,000 tonnes of British steel, and 18,000 tonnes imported from Germany they were out of the door before you could say "How big do you want your name on the shirt?" Whoops.

84 Hong Kong Eric

Cantona helps "kick racism out of football"

Eric Cantona, the mercurial French striker idolised by many, despised by quite a few, had always been somewhat unpredictable. But no-one, absolutely no-one, could have expected what he did at Selhurst Park in January 1995.

Having been sent off (again) Cantona was making his way along the touchline when a Palace "fan" ran screaming from his seat to share his opinions on Eric, his mother and the French race. Incensed, Cantona reacted by launching a two-footed kung-fu style kick at the supporter. Sacre bleu! (Or maybe Hai-ya!).

A nation watched open-mouthed and Eric was subsequently banned and almost jailed.

85 The Scorpion King
Rene Higuita's amazing clearance

Sometimes, as a journalist, a 0–0 draw can be a difficult match to report on. No goals to describe can leave you flailing around looking for one small incident to focus on. Just one little unusual detail... like perhaps a goalkeeper doing the most outrageous acrobatic clearance in the history of the game. Yes, England v Colombia's friendly at Wembley may have been a dull 0–0 but did you see that kick?! For some reason best known to himself, Colombia keeper Rene Higuita decided to clear a high ball by diving under it, flipping his legs behind him and scorpion-like, flicking it clear. He may have pointlessly risked conceding an embarrassing goal but in playgrounds (and offices) up and down the country people were doing themselves an injury for months after trying to repeat what they'd seen.

Money matters

The Bosman ruling makes a lot of agents rich

In 1986 a little known Belgian player, Jean-Marc Bosman, made history and changed football forever.

Bosman was unhappy when his club RC Liege blocked his transfer to a French club after his contract had ended.

The Belgian promptly took Liege, the Belgian FA and UEFA to the European Court of Justice in Luxembourg. The court ruled that clubs could not charge a transfer fee for players whose contracts had expired. Overnight, clubs had

to sign their players to longer, more lucrative contracts or risk losing their prize assets for nothing if they decided to "do a Bosman" at the end of their current deal.

Agents could make big money negotiating the bigger contracts or touting their players around for large signing-on fees.

So everyone was happy. Apart from the clubs, the game, and the fans. But congratulations to the agents. You can still hear the clink of their champagne glasses now.

87

Almost coming home

Euro 96 re-ignited the nation's passion for the game...

Not since 1966 had the nation been quite so behind the England team. As the hosts for Euro 96, there was a barely-contained optimism (actually, forget the barely, the optimism was *rampant*) that football really was coming home and England would win the tournament. Skinner and Baddiel's "Three Lions" song became the unofficial national anthem and football fever gripped the country. Was it blind faith? Well, as the song says: "30 years of hurt never stopped us dreaming…"

The biggest gate of the tournament, 76,864, squeezed in between the ever so slightly tatty twin towers of Wembley to watch the England v Scotland match. England were leading 1–0 with 13 minutes remaining when the Scots got a penalty. As McAllister ran up to take it, the ball appeared to bobble on the spot and Seaman saved. Surprisingly, the normally publicity-shy Uri Geller claimed credit for the shifting ball.

"Three Lions" fever reached, er, fever pitch with England's stunning (and almost surreal) 4–1 destruction of Holland. At one point the England players were, literally, queuing up to score against the Dutch. Hey, we really are going to win this tournament!

Oh bugger. Our chances of winning the tournament decrease somewhat after Germany beat us on penalties in the semi-final. They go on to take the trophy. Still, Gareth Southgate's penalty miss does at least earn him a lucrative gig starring in a pizza advert.

The 1996/97 goal of the season competition was hardly what you would call suspenseful. (Unless you were very stupid.) Because everyone knew who was going to win it when the season was only one day old. Some bloke called David Beckham…

The young Becks made the first of what would be a lifetime of headlines with an outrageous lob from just inside his own half in injury time of the match between Manchester United and Wimbledon. United were already 2–0 up when Beckham decided to try his luck, leaning back and belting the ball some 57 yards. A back-tracking Neil Sullivan could only forlornly leap too late as the ball hit the back of his net. The next day's papers had their headlines and the tabloids had a new plaything. It was the beginning of a beautiful (if occasionally turbulent) relationship.

89 He's an old hand...

Shilton makes his 1,000th appearance

You don't have to be mad to be a goalkeeper but... um, it is okay to be quite old. Peter Shilton made his first appearance in a green jersey (they all wore green back then, don't you know?) in 1966. Some 30 years later he stepped out at Brisbane Road for Third Division Leyton Orient to rack up his 1,000th League game and bag himself a place in the *Guinness Book of Records*.

The 47-year-old's career had taken in over half a dozen clubs and 125 appearances for England but the old geezer still managed to keep a clean sheet in match number 1,000. Mostly by waving a stick at opposing strikers and telling them to keep out of his allotment. Sorry, penalty area.

Who hates David Beckham? Er, everyone if you believed the national press. In a particularly spectacular version of their regular build 'em up and knock 'em down game, the papers went to town on the boy David after he got himself sent off in England's crucial second round match with Argentina in the 1998 World Cup.

A petulant, but harmless, kick at Simeone drew a red card (and some very impressive theatrics from the Argentinian). The dramatic match, which also saw a great goal by Owen and a penalty shoot-out at the end, ended with England's exit from the tournament. An effigy of Beckham was hung in East London and his face became the bullseye in a tabloid newspaper's dartboard illustration. Manager Hoddle's "defence" of his midfielder ("I'm not denying he cost us the game") didn't help and Becks became Public Enemy Number One... for a while.

Another tournament "highlight" included the Romanian team bleaching their hair blond in a rather bizarre show of team spirit. There was also Blanc kissing Barthez's bald bonce every game (ye-uck!) and Ronaldo's name disappearing and reappearing on the team sheet for the final – which hosts France won.

ADDED TIME!

Twist and shout

Ryan Giggs celebrates scoring the best FA Cup goal ever

"He gives defenders twisted blood," remarked Alex Ferguson once about Ryan Giggs' ability to turn opposition players inside out. After the 1999 FA Cup semi-final replay, there were more than a few Arsenal players who would have agreed (if they hadn't, of course, been busy receiving blood transfusions at the time…).

In a match packed with drama (Beckham's magnificent opener, Bergkamp's equaliser, Keane's sending-off, Schmeichel's penalty save) and steeped in significance (both Arsenal and United could still achieve a League and Cup double), there was little to separate the two best teams in the country.

Until Giggs collected a stray Arsenal pass in his own half, and proceeded to run the length of the pitch, dribble round the entire Arsenal defence (twice) and slam the ball into the roof of the net.

Impressively, he still had the energy to celebrate the winner by taking his shirt off and waving it around his head, in the process displaying one of the hairiest chests in football history.

Heart of glass
On-loan keeper saves Carlisle

There's leaving it late and then there's leaving it late. Carlisle, it can safely be said, left it late. Their 71-year stay in the Football League was, approximately, five seconds from coming to an end and they still needed to score one more goal to stave off Conference football. Cue on-loan keeper Jimmy Glass. Up for the final corner of the match he collected a clearance and thumped it into the net. Carlisle were safe.

Asked if this meant he would stay at the club, Glass rather smartly replied: "Who knows? Anything can happen in football – let's face it, I just got the winner!"

93 Make mine a treble
Manchester United win the lot

They called it the impossible treble but in 1999, Manchester United were making the impossible seem, well, possible. They beat Arsenal in an FA Cup semi-final replay with 10 men and a miracle Giggs goal; they came back in Turin from 2–0 down to win 3–2 against Juventus in the Champions League; they won the title race on the last day of the season with a makeshift defence, and the FA Cup after losing their skipper Roy Keane through injury. Now all they had to do was win the European Cup... naturally, they did it the hard way.

Without Scholes and Keane, and with Giggs playing out of position, it was a lacklustre United performance in the Nou Camp against Bayern Munich. The Germans took the lead after just five minutes and some 85 minutes later, with United looking incapable of even creating a chance, the officials had already tied Bayern's colours to the trophy.

The game went into stoppage time and now, a comeback looked completely impossible. So, United, of course came back. Three minutes and two corners later United were European champions in the most dramatic fashion imaginable.

Fortunately, there was just time to tie on the correct ribbons.

Reds dance upon the Rio sands

United swap FA Cup romance for Copacabana sun

The 1999 Treble winners Manchester United's chances of immediately repeating their Treble success in 2000 were dashed somewhat when they didn't enter one of the three competitions.

To ensure England's bid to stage the 2006 World Cup would be successful, the Premiership champions were persuaded to play in the FIFA Club World Championship. FIFA chiefs cleverly scheduled the exciting new tournament right in the middle of the English season thus ensuring United would not be able to play in the passé 128-year old FA Cup going on back at home.

It was a brilliant idea, a tournament in Rio (with easy access to the Copacabana beach) that brought together all the great clubs in the world from Raja Casablanca to Al-Nassr and, yes, even South Melbourne!

The 2,000 fans who crammed into the 73,000-capacity Maracana Stadium for United's first match against Mexican giants Necaxa clearly agreed it was the birth of a football revolution. What (an) atmosphere.

United's cold-weather training quickly paid off as they drew one, lost one and won only one of their group matches to ensure immediate elimination and maximum beach time.

The FIFA Club World Championship wasn't repeated, England won't stage the 2006 World Cup and Manchester United players hardly won a game of head tennis on Copacabana beach. It was a sunny new dawn for football.

MANCHESTER UNITED

Roy of the Wanderers
Hastily-acquired striker proves the hero

Ah, the romance of the Cup. Ignore what you just read on the left. In 2001, Wycombe Wanderers proved that the modern game hasn't yet lost *all* its charms as they reached the semi-finals of the competition. The hero of the hour was Roy Essandoh, an until then very unfamous striker who rumour has it was bought off the internet when all Wycombe's first team forwards got injured.

He struck the crucial quarter-final winner against Leicester that earned the Wanderers a place in the last four against Liverpool and reminded everyone just why the FA Cup remains a jewel in the sporting crown. (The club later denied they'd bought Roy off the internet – they said they found him on teletext. Ah, well that's all right then…).

Swede thrown into hotpot

Uproar as Sven becomes England's first foreign manager

On 7 October 2000, England lost their first World Cup 2002 qualifying match (and the final game ever to be played at Wembley). To Germany! More importantly though, the man they once called "Super Kev" (and "Mighty Mouse" and "Bubble Head") resigned as England manager claiming his tactics weren't super enough to do the job.

It was time for a change, and the FA made a decision that would drop a bespectacled Swede in the stewing pot of English football. Yes, they appointed Sven-Göran Eriksson – a FOREIGNER!

Media pundits and football legends were united in horror. Former England defender (and Republic of Ireland manager) Jack Charlton captured the prevailing mood describing the FA's decision as "a terrible mistake".

Indeed, why give the job to an inexperienced foreigner who'd only won the Italian league, European Cup Winners Cup and Super Cup with Lazio, three Portuguese league titles with Benfica, and a Swedish championship and a Uefa Cup with IFK Gothenburg (among other trophies). What about Alan Curbishley, John Gregory and, er, Barry Fry? The rookie Swede was surely set to join former England boss Graham "Turnip" Taylor in the tabloids' vegetable patch.

Only six flukey World Cup qualifying wins in a row postponed Sven's date with composting destiny.

97

5-1!
England thump Germany in World Cup qualifier

Alois Alzheimer, Nadja Auermann, Andreas Baader, Johann Sebastian Bach, Ludwig van Beethoven, Boris Becker, Karl Benz, 'Bix' Beiderbecke, Bertolt Brecht, Otto von Bismarck, Adi Dassler, Gottfried Daimler, Marlene Dietrich, Albert Einstein, Gabriel Daniel Fahrenheit, H.R. Giger, Steffi Graf, Günter Grass, Franz Joseph Haydn, Heinrich Rudolf Hertz, Henry A. Kissinger, Helmut Kohl, Karl Lagerfeld, Hedy Lamarr, Karl Marx, George Simon Ohm, Wolfgang Petersen, Erwin Rommel, Claudia Schiffer, Albert Schweitzer, Wim Wenders, Ferdinand von Zeppelin, Hans Zimmer… your boys took one hell of a beating!

Big Ron: A celebration
The man who, er, re-invented commentary

Once in every generation, there comes a man who raises the bar in his chosen field. In the field of football commentary that bar-raiser is Big Ron Bo Jangles Atkinson (to use his full title).

Big Ron's verbal dexterity was wasted as a football manager/sun-worshipper, and it was only when he grabbed the mic to Clive Tyldesley that his gift was revealed to the wider world and beyond

To choose just one momentous Ron-ism would be churlish. The concise analogies (on Paul Scholes: "The boy's a bubble") the controversial claims ("Zero-zero is a big score"), the appreciation of time and space ("He had acres of time there"), the factual insights ("They are playing above ground") and the penetrating rhetorical questions ("How are they defensively, attacking-wise?") ...all these qualities have combined to make Big Ron indisputably "The Ron" of modern football commentators.

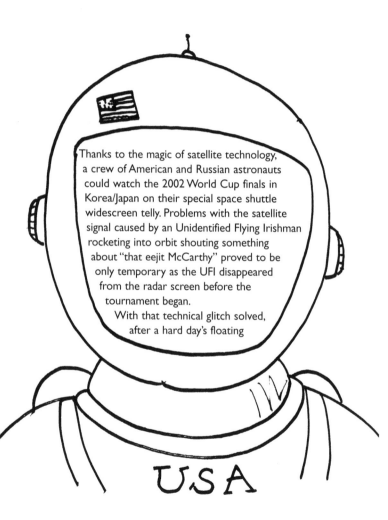

Thanks to the magic of satellite technology, a crew of American and Russian astronauts could watch the 2002 World Cup finals in Korea/Japan on their special space shuttle widescreen telly. Problems with the satellite signal caused by an Unidentified Flying Irishman rocketing into orbit shouting something about "that eejit McCarthy" proved to be only temporary as the UFI disappeared from the radar screen before the tournament began.

With that technical glitch solved, after a hard day's floating

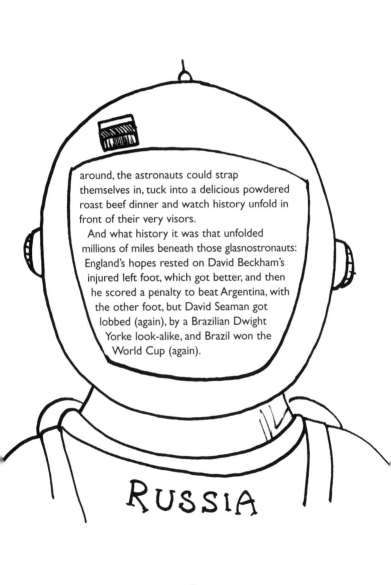

around, the astronauts could strap themselves in, tuck into a delicious powdered roast beef dinner and watch history unfold in front of their very visors.

And what history it was that unfolded millions of miles beneath those glasnostronauts: England's hopes rested on David Beckham's injured left foot, which got better, and then he scored a penalty to beat Argentina, with the other foot, but David Seaman got lobbed (again), by a Brazilian Dwight Yorke look-alike, and Brazil won the World Cup (again).

RUSSIA

September Week 36 2003

4 Thursday

We're staying in a place called Skippy or summat like that. It's city in a country that used to be in Yugoslavia but has moved to Macedonia. The hotel is all right, but room service ain't great. I rung down for a couple of meat pies, sausages and chips for me tea, just like me mam makes, but the bloke who took my order didn't hear me right. He sounded a bit Swedish. They sent up a fookin' chicken salad instead. I'm starvin'.

5 Friday

We did shooting practice in training today and had a good laugh. Emile's a real joker. He was hitting shots out of the ground again and again. Still hungry. I rang me agent to ask if he could fly in some food from Kenny Po's chinese in Croxteth. Could murder some sweet and sour pork balls. A lot of the boys have got these multi-coloured watches and I'm thinking of buying one. They are like Swatch watches but cost ten grand (or 35K if you want diamonds in it like Becks). Brilliant.

On 6 September 2003, manchild boy wonder Wayne Rooney became the youngest player ever to score for England at 17 years and 318 days old, beating the now old Michael Owen's previous record

6 Saturday

Rang Colleen in the morning. She wished me luck for the match against Maccy D. I love her so much, I've got a tattoo with her name on it on me arm. Jamesy told me it was illegal, cos you are not allowed to tattoo a miner. I think he was joking cos I'm a footballer, not a friggin' miner.

In the match, we woz crap in the first half and went 1-0 down. Emile came on for Lamps at half-time and all the shooting practice paid off for him when he headed it to me and I scored the equaliser.

Then Becks made it 2-1 so we won. Wicked!

7 Sunday

Back in England. In the papers it says that people are starting a Monster Raving Rooney Party. Not sure I want to be a politician yet though – I'm just concentrating on me football. One of me mates rang up and invited me out for a Sunday roast, but we've got another match against Lickingties on Wednesday so I'll stick with the squad. Also, I've got to plan my 18th birthday party. Me pal Robbie says he will sing a few of his karaoke songs if I give him a signed shirt. Cheeky bugger.

ROONY

101 Ab Fab
Roman Abramovich turns Chelsea into Chelski

Money can't buy you love (well maybe monkey love) but it can buy you a football team! And success! Probably! Or at least that's what Roman Abramovich is hoping he's going to get for the several billion pounds (roughly) that he's so far spent on turning Chelsea (sorry, Chelski as *everyone* calls them these days) into Champions home and abroad.

The Russian billionaire is hoping to achieve footballing alchemy by combining vast sums of cash, Claudio Ranieri's strange tactical decisions and, er, John Terry. And the scary thing is, he's only just starting. As another of our astonishing exclusives exclusively reveals (see Roman's desktop below) he's planning to spend even more. It all seems a long way from villagers chasing a ball down the street. Which is fair enough, as that was 900 years ago.

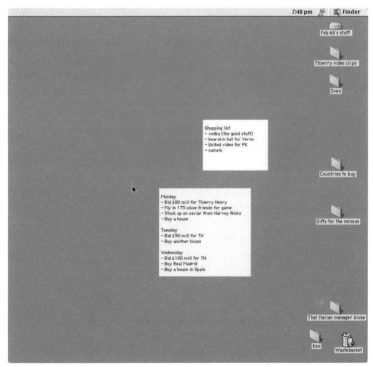